TABLE OF CONTENTS

Silent Night

SOLO OR
1st ACCORDION (EASY)

GRUBER
Arr. Palmer-Hughes

Si - lent night! Ho - ly night!

* When this selection is played as a band number PLAY RIGHT HAND 8va, with BANDONEON.

SILENT NIGHT

SOLO OR
1st ACCORDION (ADVANCED)

GRUBER
Arr. Palmer-Hughes

SILENT NIGHT

2nd ACCORDION

SILENT NIGHT

Up On The House-Top

SOLO OR
1st ACCORDION (EASY)

HANBY
Arr. Palmer-Hughes

OBOE
Up on the house-top rein-deer pause, Out jumps good old Sant-a Claus;

TENOR
Down thro' the chim-ney with lots of toys, All for the chil-dren, Christ-mas joys.

Ho, Ho, Ho! who wouldn't go? Ho, Ho, Ho! who wouldn't go?

MASTER
Up on the house-top, Click, Click, Click, Down thro' the chim-ney with good Saint Nick!

UP ON THE HOUSE-TOP

SOLO OR
1st ACCORDION (ADVANCED)

HANBY
Arr. Palmer-Hughes

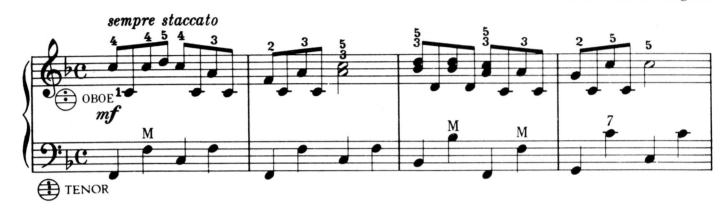

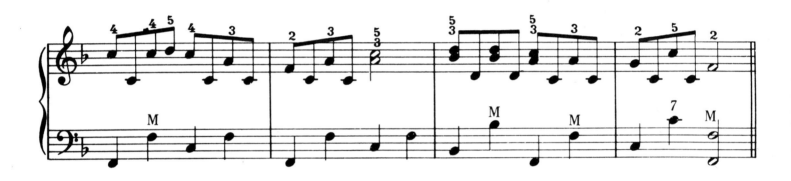

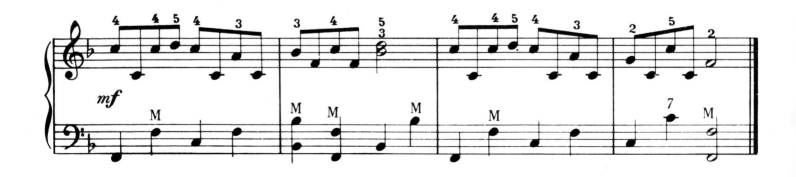

UP ON THE HOUSE - TOP

Jingle Bells

These bells are shaken in rhythm
as indicated by the "notes" (✗)
in the music.

ELASTIC

For playing this novelty arrangement, each player should be equipped with a band of Christmas bells, worn just above the wrist, on the right arm. Such bands may be purchased or easily made with bells that are available at all ten-cent stores.

SOLO OR
1st ACCORDION (EASY)

TRADITIONAL
Arr. Palmer-Hughes

Christmas bells:

Verse

Refrain

*WHEN THIS SELECTION IS PLAYED AS A BAND NUMBER, PLAY RIGHT HAND 8va, WITH FULL REGISTER ⊕ MASTER

JINGLE BELLS

SOLO OR
1st ACCORDION (ADVANCED)

TRADITIONAL
Arr. Palmer-Hughes

Verse

Dash – ing thro' the snow in a one horse o – pen sleigh

O'er the fields we go laugh – ing all the way.

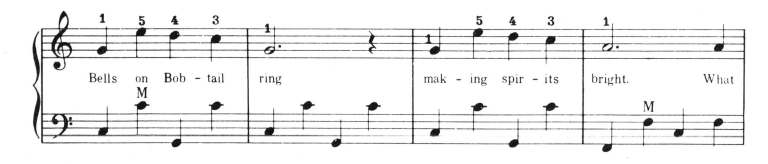

Bells on Bob – tail ring mak – ing spir – its bright. What

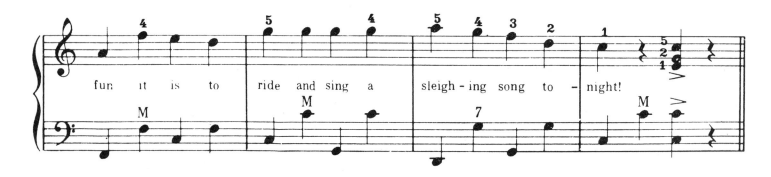

fun it is to ride and sing a sleigh – ing song to – night!

Refrain

JINGLE BELLS

2nd ACCORDION

JINGLE BELLS

3rd ACCORDION

16

JINGLE BELLS

4th ACCORDION

O Little Town Of Bethlehem

SOLO OR
1st ACCORDION (EASY)

BROOKS - REDNER
Arr. Palmer-Hughes

VERY IMPORTANT!
*When this selection is played as a band number THIS PART
must be played RIGHT HAND ONLY, 8va ⊕ THROUGHOUT

O LITTLE TOWN OF BETHLEHEM

SOLO OR
1st ACCORDION (ADVANCED)

BROOKS - REDNER
Arr. Palmer-Hughes

USE A♭
BELOW E♭

2nd ACCORDION

O LITTLE TOWN OF BETHLEHEM

3rd ACCORDION

4th ACCORDION

5th ACCORDION

HARK! THE HERALD ANGELS SING

SOLO OR
1st ACCORDION (ADVANCED)

WESLEY - MENDELSSOHN
Arr. Palmer-Hughes

2nd ACCORDION

HARK! THE HERALD ANGELS SING

O Come All Ye Faithful

SOLO OR
1st ACCORDION (EASY)

TRADITIONAL
Arr. Palmer-Hughes

MASTER *f* O Come all ye faith-ful joy-ful and tri - um-phant, oh come ye, oh come ye to Beth - le - hem. Come and be - hold Him born the King of an - gels O come let us a - dore Him, O come let us a - dore Him, O come let us a - dore Him Christ the Lord.

VERY IMPORTANT!
When this selection is played as a band number
THIS PART must be played RIGHT HAND ONLY, 8va.

O COME ALL YE FAITHFUL

SOLO OR
1st ACCORDION (ADVANCED)

TRADITIONAL
Arr. Palmer-Hughes

2nd ACCORDION

O COME ALL YE FAITHFUL

IT CAME UPON THE MIDNIGHT CLEAR

SOLO OR
1st ACCORDION (EASY)

SEARS –WILLIS
Arr. Palmer-Hughes

> **VERY IMPORTANT!**
> When this selection is played as a band number
> THIS PART must be played RIGHT HAND ONLY, 8va.

IT CAME UPON THE MIDNIGHT CLEAR

SOLO OR
1st ACCORDION (ADVANCED)

SEARS - WILLIS
Arr. Palmer-Hughes

IT CAME UPON THE MIDNIGHT CLEAR

2nd ACCORDION

3rd ACCORDION

IT CAME UPON THE MIDNIGHT CLEAR

We Three Kings Of Orient Are

SOLO OR
1st ACCORDION (EASY)

HOPKINS
Arr. Palmer-Hughes

Lyrics under the music:

We three Kings of O - ri - ent are, bear - ing gifts we tra-verse a - far. Field and foun - tain, moor and moun - tain, fol-low-ing yon - der star. O star of won - der star of night star with roy - al beau - ty bright. West - ward lead - ing still pro - ceed - ing Guide us to thy per - fect light.

> **VERY IMPORTANT!**
> When this selection is played as a band number
> THIS PART must be played RIGHT HAND ONLY, 8va.

WE THREE KINGS OF ORIENT ARE

SOLO OR
1st ACCORDION (ADVANCED)

HOPKINS
Arr. Palmer-Hughes

WE THREE KINGS OF ORIENT ARE

2nd ACCORDION

WE THREE KINGS OF ORIENT ARE

Joy To The World

SOLO OR
1st ACCORDION (EASY)

WATTS - HANDEL
Arr. Palmer-Hughes

VERY IMPORTANT!
* When this selection is played as a band number
THIS PART must be played RIGHT HAND ONLY, 8va.

JOY TO THE WORLD

SOLO OR
1st ACCORDION (ADVANCED)

WATTS - HANDEL
Arr. Palmer-Hughes

2nd ACCORDION

JOY TO THE WORLD

WHAT CHILD IS THIS?

(GREENSLEEVES)

SOLO OR
1st ACCORDION (ADVANCED)

TRADITIONAL
Arr. Palmer-Hughes

WHAT CHILD IS THIS?

(GREENSLEEVES)

2nd ACCORDION

3rd ACCORDION

WHAT CHILD IS THIS?
(GREENSLEEVES)

ANGELS WE HAVE HEARD ON HIGH

SOLO OR
1st ACCORDION (EASY)

TRADITIONAL
Arr. Palmer-Hughes

VERY IMPORTANT!
When this selection is played as a band number
THIS PART must be played RIGHT HAND ONLY, 8va.

ANGELS WE HAVE HEARD ON HIGH

SOLO OR
1st ACCORDION (ADVANCED)

TRADITIONAL
Arr. Palmer-Hughes

ANGELS WE HAVE HEARD ON HIGH

ANGELS WE HAVE HEARD ON HIGH

How Brightly Shines The Morning Star

SOLO OR
1st ACCORDION (EASY)

NICOLAI - BACH
Arr. Palmer-Hughes

VERY IMPORTANT!
When this selection is played as a band number
THIS PART must be played RIGHT HAND ONLY, 8va.

HOW BRIGHTLY SHINES THE MORNING STAR

NICOLAI - BACH
Arr. Palmer-Hughes

SOLO OR
1st ACCORDION (ADVANCED)

HOW BRIGHTLY SHINES THE MORNING STAR

HOW BRIGHTLY SHINES THE MORNING STAR